Title

Ecommerce Entrepreneurship: A Step-by-Step Guide for Beginners

Author
Deepak Kumar

Table of Contents:

About author

Deepak Kumar, a graduate in Commerce, embarked on his entrepreneurial journey at the age of 22 in India. Leveraging his profound understanding of business dynamics, he adeptly initiated and developed two successful online brands from their inception. Demonstrating expertise in brand building, marketing, and fostering growth, Mr. Kumar has accumulated valuable insights through hands-on experience.

Motivated by a passion for imparting knowledge, he has transitioned into an author, sharing his wealth of expertise through the medium of books. Additionally, Mr. Kumar extends his insights to personalized one-on-one consultations, contributing to the mentorship and guidance of aspiring entrepreneurs and business enthusiasts.

"Welcome to the digital journey – where possibilities unfold with knowledge."

Chapter 1
Introduction to E-commerce

Welcome to the transformative world of e-commerce, where digital innovation converges with traditional commerce, reshaping the way businesses operate and consumers shop. In this comprehensive exploration, we will delve into the multifaceted dimensions of e-commerce, from understanding its diverse definitions and types to unravelling the advantages of starting an e-commerce business. Additionally, we will examine the dynamic market trends and opportunities that characterize this ever-evolving landscape.

1. Understanding E-commerce

E-commerce, short for electronic commerce, fundamentally refers to the buying and selling of goods and services over the internet. This digital exchange eliminates geographical constraints and enables businesses to reach a global audience. The realm of e-commerce is vast, encompassing various types and models that cater to diverse consumer needs and market dynamics.

1.1 Definition and Types of E-commerce

Definition of E-commerce:

At its core, e-commerce, or electronic commerce, refers to the buying and selling of goods and services over the internet. This shift from traditional brick-and-mortar retail has spawned various types of e-commerce, each catering to specific needs and preferences.

Types of E-commerce:

1. Business-to-Consumer (B2C): This is the most common form, where businesses sell products or services directly to end consumers. Examples include online retail stores, travel websites, and subscription services.

2. Business-to-Business (B2B): In B2B e-commerce, transactions occur between businesses. This includes wholesale trade, where one business sells products or services to another for resale or internal use.

3. Consumer-to-Consumer (C2C): C2C e-commerce involves transactions between individual consumers. Online marketplaces and platforms that facilitate peer-to-peer transactions fall under this category.

4. Consumer-to-Business (C2B): In C2B, individuals sell products or offer services to businesses. This model is often associated with freelancers, influencers, or individuals with specific expertise.

5. Mobile Commerce (M-commerce): M-commerce refers to e-commerce transactions conducted through mobile devices. This includes mobile banking, in-app purchases, and mobile-friendly online stores.

6. Social Commerce: Social commerce integrates e-commerce with social media platforms, allowing users to make purchases directly through social channels. It leverages the social network for product discovery and recommendations.

Understanding the diverse types of e-commerce provides a foundation for entrepreneurs and businesses to identify the most suitable model based on their products, target audience, and business goals.

1.2 Advantages of Starting an E-commerce Business

The decision to embark on an e-commerce venture is often fuelled by the numerous advantages it offers to entrepreneurs and businesses alike. Understanding these benefits is crucial for making informed decisions and leveraging the full potential of the digital marketplace.

Advantages of E-commerce:

1. Global Reach: E-commerce transcends geographical boundaries, allowing businesses to reach a global audience without the constraints of physical locations.

2. 24/7 Availability: Online stores operate 24/7, providing customers with the flexibility to browse and make purchases at any time, enhancing convenience.

3. Cost-Efficiency: E-commerce eliminates the need for physical storefronts, reducing overhead costs associated with rent, utilities, and maintenance.

4. Targeted Marketing: Digital marketing tools enable businesses to target specific audiences based on demographics, interests, and online behaviour, enhancing the efficiency of marketing campaigns.

5. Data-driven Insights: E-commerce platforms provide valuable data and analytics, offering insights into customer behaviour, preferences, and buying patterns for informed decision-making.

6. Scalability: E-commerce businesses can easily scale operations by expanding product offerings, reaching new markets, and adapting to changing demands.

7. Improved Customer Experience: Online platforms allow for personalized customer experiences, from tailored recommendations to efficient customer support through chat and email.

8. Inventory Management: Digital platforms streamline inventory management, reducing the risk of overstock or stockouts with real-time tracking and analytics.

1.3 Market Trends and Opportunities

The e-commerce landscape is dynamic, shaped by emerging trends and evolving consumer preferences. Staying attuned to market trends is essential for businesses to seize opportunities and stay competitive.

Current Market Trends:

1. Rise of Omnichannel Retail: Integration of online and offline channels to provide a seamless shopping experience, allowing customers to switch between physical stores and digital platforms.

2. Mobile Shopping Dominance: The increasing use of smartphones for online shopping has propelled mobile commerce to the forefront, emphasizing the need for mobile-friendly platforms.

3. E-commerce Personalization: Tailoring online experiences based on individual preferences, purchase history, and behaviour to enhance customer engagement and satisfaction.

4. Voice Commerce: The adoption of voice-activated devices has given rise to voice commerce, where customers make purchases using virtual assistants like Alexa or Google Assistant.

5. Sustainable E-commerce Practices: Consumers are increasingly prioritizing sustainable and eco-friendly products, driving e-commerce businesses to embrace environmentally conscious practices.

6. Augmented Reality (AR) and Virtual Reality (VR): Integration of AR and VR technologies for immersive online shopping experiences, allowing customers to visualize products before purchasing.

Opportunities in E-commerce:

1. Niche Market Exploration: Identifying and catering to specific niche markets that may be underserved in the e-commerce landscape.

2. Subscription-based Models: Offering subscription services for products or curated experiences, providing a steady revenue stream and customer loyalty.

3. Cross-border E-commerce: Exploring opportunities in international markets by overcoming logistical challenges and adapting to diverse consumer preferences.

4. Innovative Payment Solutions: Integrating new and secure payment options, such as cryptocurrency or digital wallets, to cater to diverse customer preferences.

5. Collaborations and Partnerships: Collaborating with influencers, other businesses, or online platforms to expand reach and tap into new customer bases.

Understanding current market trends and exploring diverse opportunities positions e-commerce entrepreneurs to adapt, innovate, and thrive in the ever-evolving digital marketplace.

In the subsequent chapters, we will continue our exploration of e-commerce, diving into strategies for effective online store management, digital marketing best practices, and the integration of emerging technologies. The journey into the heart of e-commerce continues, offering insights and guidance for those seeking success in this dynamic and transformative domain.

Chapter 2
Finding Your Niche

In the vast and ever-expanding world of e-commerce, discovering the right niche is a pivotal step towards building a successful and sustainable online business. This chapter delves into the intricacies of finding your niche, from identifying your passion and expertise to conducting market research, analysing competitors, and ultimately making informed decisions about the niche that aligns with your goals and aspirations.

2.1 Identifying Your Passion and Expertise

Embarking on an e-commerce journey begins with a deep exploration of your own passions and expertise. Finding a niche that resonates with your interests not only fuels your motivation but also positions you as an authority in the field. Consider the following aspects:

Passion Mapping:

1. **Personal Interests:** Identify subjects or hobbies that genuinely captivate your interest.

2. **Skills and Talents:** Assess your skills and talents, exploring how they can be translated into a viable niche.

3. Problem Solving: Reflect on problems you are passionate about solving, as this can lead to niche ideas with a purpose.

Expertise Assessment:

1. Professional Background: Consider your professional experiences and expertise, as they can guide you towards niches where you already possess knowledge.

2. Educational Background: Assess your educational background for areas where you have acquired specialized knowledge.

3. Networking: Tap into your network and seek feedback on areas where others perceive your expertise.

2.2 Researching Market Demand

While passion and expertise are crucial, aligning your niche with market demand ensures there's a viable customer base eager for your offerings. Conduct thorough market research to gauge the demand for your potential niche:

Market Research Steps:

1. Keyword Analysis: Use tools like Google Keyword Planner to identify search volumes related to your niche.

2. Competitor Analysis: Examine existing businesses in your proposed niche to understand their success and shortcomings.

3. Consumer Surveys: Create surveys or polls to directly gather insights from potential customers.

4. Industry Reports: Explore industry reports and publications for trends and growth projections.

5. Social Media Trends: Monitor social media platforms to identify trending topics and discussions.

2.3 Analysing Competitors

A comprehensive analysis of competitors provides invaluable insights into market dynamics and potential strategies. Understand the strengths and weaknesses of existing players in your niche:

Competitor Analysis Framework:

1. Identify Competitors: List direct and indirect competitors within your niche.

2. SWOT Analysis: Evaluate their Strengths, Weaknesses, Opportunities, and Threats.

3. Pricing Strategies: Analyse how competitors price their products or services.

4. Customer Reviews: Scrutinize customer reviews to identify common pain points and areas for improvement.

5. Unique Selling Proposition (USP): Identify the unique elements that set competitors apart.

2.4 Choosing the Right Niche for You

Armed with insights from passion assessment, market demand research, and competitor analysis, the final step is making an informed decision on the right niche for your e-commerce venture:

Decision-Making Criteria:

1. Alignment with Passion: Ensure your chosen niche aligns with your personal interests and passion.

2. Market Potential: Choose a niche with sufficient market demand, indicated by keyword research and competitor analysis.

3. Competitive Advantage: Identify ways you can differentiate your business within the chosen niche.

4. Scalability: Assess the scalability of the niche to accommodate future business growth.

5. Long-Term Viability: Consider the long-term sustainability and relevance of the chosen niche.

In conclusion, finding your niche in the e-commerce landscape is a meticulous process that combines introspection, market research, competitor analysis, and strategic decision-making. By aligning your business with your passions, addressing market demand, understanding competitors, and making informed choices, you set the foundation for a thriving e-commerce venture. In the subsequent chapters, we will explore how to turn your niche into a profitable online business, covering aspects such as product selection, branding, and marketing strategies.

Chapter 3
Market Research and Validation

In the dynamic landscape of e-commerce, thorough market research and validation are critical steps in ensuring the viability and success of your business idea. This chapter guides you through the comprehensive process of conducting market research, defining your target audience, validating your product or service, and refining your business idea to meet the needs of your prospective customers.

3.1 Conducting Market Research

Market research serves as the foundation for informed decision-making, helping you understand market dynamics, customer behavior, and potential challenges. Follow these steps to conduct effective market research:

Understanding Market Trends:

1. Industry Analysis: Examine the broader industry to identify trends, challenges, and opportunities.

2. Market Size: Determine the size of your target market to gauge its potential.

3. Growth Projections: Explore industry reports and forecasts to understand the future trajectory of your market.

4. Regulatory Environment: Be aware of any regulations or legal considerations that may impact your business.

Consumer Behavior Analysis:

1. Consumer Needs: Identify the needs and preferences of your target audience.

2. Buying Patterns: Analyze how and when your target customers make purchasing decisions.

3. Pain Points: Understand the challenges and pain points your potential customers face.

Competitor Analysis:

1. Identify Competitors: List direct and indirect competitors operating in your niche.

2. SWOT Analysis: Evaluate the strengths, weaknesses, opportunities, and threats associated with each competitor.

3. Product Offerings: Scrutinize the products or services offered by competitors, identifying gaps or areas for improvement.

Market Research Tools:

1. Surveys and Questionnaires: Gather direct feedback from potential customers through surveys.

2. Google Trends: Explore trending topics and search queries related to your niche.

3. Social Media Listening: Monitor social media platforms for discussions, reviews, and sentiments related to your industry.

3.2 Defining Your Target Audience

Understanding and defining your target audience is a crucial aspect of market research. Tailor your products and marketing strategies to resonate with the specific needs and preferences of your ideal customers:

Creating Customer Personas:

1. Demographic Information: Define the age, gender, location, and income level of your target audience.

2. Psychographic Factors: Explore lifestyle choices, values, and interests that define your ideal customers.

3. Behavioral Patterns: Understand how your target audience behaves, their preferences, and buying habits.

Segmentation and Targeting:

1. Segmentation Criteria: Identify criteria for segmenting your audience based on relevant factors.

2. Targeting Strategies: Tailor your products and marketing messages to appeal to specific segments within your audience.

3. Positioning: Determine how your brand and offerings will be positioned in the minds of your target customers.

3.3 Validating Your Product or Service

Validation ensures that there is a genuine demand for your product or service in the market. It involves testing your business idea before full-scale implementation:

Minimum Viable Product (MVP):

1. MVP Development: Create a simplified version of your product or service to test its appeal.

2. Feedback Gathering: Collect feedback from a select group of potential customers to refine your offering.

3. Iterative Improvement: Use feedback to iterate and improve your MVP, ensuring it aligns with customer expectations.

Pilot Testing:

1. Limited Launch: Introduce your product or service on a smaller scale to gauge market response.

2. Performance Evaluation: Assess customer reactions, sales, and any challenges encountered during the pilot phase.

3. Adjustments and Optimization: Make necessary adjustments based on the insights gained from the pilot testing.

3.4 Refining Your Business Idea

The refinement process involves synthesizing insights from market research and validation to shape your business idea into a more robust and market-ready proposition:

Iterative Process:

1. Feedback Analysis: Thoroughly analyze feedback from market research, target audience definition, and product validation.

2. Adjustment and Enhancement: Make necessary adjustments to your business idea, considering areas for enhancement.

3. Value Proposition Refinement: Refine your value proposition based on customer needs, preferences, and competitive differentiators.

Iterative Testing:

1. Continuous Improvement: Adopt a mindset of continuous improvement, regularly testing and refining your business idea.

2. Adaptability: Stay adaptable and responsive to evolving market trends and customer expectations.

3. Data-Driven Decisions: Base decisions on data and insights gathered through ongoing market research and customer feedback.

In conclusion, market research and validation are essential components of developing a successful e-commerce business. By understanding market trends, defining your target audience, validating your product or service, and iteratively refining your business idea, you pave the way for a more informed and customer-centric approach. In the subsequent chapters, we will explore strategies for product sourcing, branding, and effective marketing to bring your refined business idea to fruition in the competitive e-commerce landscape.

Chapter 4:
Creating a Business Plan

A well-crafted business plan is the cornerstone of a successful venture, providing a roadmap for entrepreneurs to navigate the complexities of business ownership. This chapter explores the significance of a business plan, delves into the key components that make it comprehensive, and guides you through the process of articulating your vision into a strategic document.

4.1 Importance of a Business Plan

A business plan is not just a document; it's a dynamic tool that serves as a compass, guiding entrepreneurs through the challenges and opportunities that lie ahead. Understanding the importance of a business plan is essential for any aspiring business owner:

Strategic Roadmap:

1. Direction and Vision: A business plan crystallizes your vision, outlining the path you intend to take with your business.

2. Goal Setting: Clearly defined objectives provide milestones to strive for, enhancing focus and accountability.

3. Risk Mitigation: Identifying potential risks and challenges allows for proactive planning and mitigation strategies.

Communication and Alignment:

1. Communication Tool: A well-communicated plan aligns stakeholders, ensuring everyone understands the business's mission and strategy.

2. Investor Attraction: For those seeking funding, a compelling business plan is often the first step to attracting investors and partners.

3. Team Alignment: Internal teams benefit from a shared understanding of the business's goals and strategies, fostering collaboration and cohesion.

Operational Efficiency:

1. Resource Allocation: Helps in efficient allocation of resources by prioritizing activities based on their impact on business objectives.

2. Performance Measurement: Establishes key performance indicators (KPIs) for monitoring and evaluating business performance.

3. Adaptability: A dynamic business plan allows for adjustments based on market changes and evolving circumstances.

4.2 Key Components of a Business Plan

Creating a business plan involves breaking down the business into comprehensive components that collectively form a cohesive strategy. Each section plays a vital role in providing a holistic view of your business:

4.2.1 Executive Summary

The executive summary serves as a snapshot of the entire business plan, summarizing key elements, goals, and strategies in a concise manner. It is often the first section potential investors and partners read, making it crucial for leaving a lasting impression.

Elements of an Executive Summary:

1. Business Name and Overview: Clearly state the business's name and provide a brief overview.

2. Mission Statement: Define the purpose and mission of the business.

3. Business Structure: Indicate the legal structure of the business (e.g., sole proprietorship, LLC, corporation).

4. Product or Service Offering: Concisely describe the core offerings of the business.

5. Target Market: Identify the primary target audience and market segment.

6. Financial Summary: Include key financial highlights such as projected revenue, expenses, and funding requirements.

4.2.2 Business Description

The business description delves into the specifics of the venture, providing a detailed narrative that expands on the information introduced in the executive summary.

Components of a Business Description:

1. History and Origin: Share the story of how the business came into existence and its historical context.

2. Vision and Goals: Articulate the long-term vision and specific goals the business aims to achieve.

3. Value Proposition: Clearly state the unique value the business offers to its customers.

4. Legal Structure: Provide details about the legal structure, ownership, and management team.

5. Location and Facilities: Outline the physical location(s) and any facilities crucial to the business operations.

6. Milestones and Achievements: Highlight significant milestones achieved and future milestones to strive for.

4.2.3 Market Analysis

A comprehensive understanding of the market is crucial for shaping business strategies and positioning the venture for success.

Components of a Market Analysis:

1. Industry Overview: Provide an overview of the industry, including trends, growth projections, and key players.

2. Target Market: Define the specific market segments and demographics the business aims to serve.

3. Competitive Analysis: Assess competitors, identifying strengths, weaknesses, opportunities, and threats.

4. SWOT Analysis: Conduct a SWOT analysis, evaluating internal strengths and weaknesses, and external opportunities and threats.

5. Customer Persona: Create detailed customer personas, outlining the characteristics and preferences of the target audience.

6. Market Trends: Highlight current and emerging trends that could impact the industry and the business.

4.2.4 Organization and Management

This section provides an in-depth view of the organizational structure and the team driving the business forward.

Elements of Organization and Management:

1. Organizational Structure: Outline the hierarchical structure of the organization, including departments and key roles.

2. Ownership Structure: Specify the ownership distribution and any equity arrangements among founders and stakeholders.

3. Management Team: Introduce key members of the management team, highlighting their roles, qualifications, and contributions.

4. Advisory Board or External Partners: If applicable, mention any external advisors or partners who contribute to the business's success.

5. Roles and Responsibilities: Clearly define the roles and responsibilities of each key team member.

4.2.5 Product or Service Line

This section provides a detailed overview of the products or services the business offers, emphasizing their unique features and benefits.

Components of Product or Service Line:

1. Product Descriptions: Detail each product or service, including specifications, features, and potential variations.

2. Differentiators: Highlight what sets the products or services apart from competitors in the market.

3. Pricing Strategy: Define the pricing strategy, taking into consideration factors such as cost, value, and market competition.

4. Product Life Cycle: Discuss the life cycle of each product or service, considering factors such as introduction, growth, maturity, and decline.

5. Intellectual Property: If applicable, detail any patents, trademarks, or other forms of intellectual property associated with the products or services.

4.2.6 Marketing and Sales

A robust marketing and sales strategy is integral to driving awareness, attracting customers, and achieving revenue goals.

Components of Marketing and Sales:

1. Marketing Strategy: Outline the overarching marketing approach, incorporating channels, tactics, and campaigns.

2. Sales Strategy: Detail the sales process, from lead generation to conversion, highlighting key milestones and strategies.

3. Customer Acquisition: Specify methods for acquiring and retaining customers, including outreach, advertising, and promotions.

4. Distribution Channels: Identify the channels through which products or services will be distributed to customers.

5. Marketing Budget: Include a budget allocation for marketing initiatives, specifying expenses for each strategy.

4.2.7 Funding Request

If seeking external funding, this section provides a transparent overview of the capital required to support business operations and achieve growth.

Elements of a Funding Request:

1. Funding Purpose: Clearly state the purpose of the funds, whether for initial startup costs, expansion, or a specific project.

2. Amount Requested: Specify the exact amount of funding required, providing a breakdown if necessary.

3. Use of Funds: Outline how the funds will be utilized, including expenses such as equipment purchase, marketing campaigns, or hiring.

4. Return on Investment (ROI): If applicable, outline the anticipated ROI for investors or lenders.

5. Terms of Funding: Specify the terms of funding, including interest rates, equity shares, or any other relevant agreements.

4.2.8 Financial Projections

Financial projections provide a forward-looking view of the business's financial performance, helping stakeholders gauge its potential profitability.

Components of Financial Projections:

1. Revenue Forecast: Outline expected revenue streams, considering factors such as pricing, sales volume, and market share.

2. Expense Forecast: Project anticipated expenses, including operational costs, marketing expenditures, and overhead.

3. Profit and Loss Statement: Present a comprehensive profit and loss statement, detailing revenue, expenses, and net income.

4. Cash Flow Statement: Project cash flow, considering the timing of income and expenses to ensure sufficient liquidity.

5. Balance Sheet: Provide a snapshot of the business's financial position, including assets, liabilities, and equity.

4.2.9 Appendix

The appendix serves as a repository for supplementary materials that support and enhance the information presented throughout the business plan.

Common Appendix Elements:

1. Additional Financial Data: Include detailed financial statements, charts, and graphs for deeper analysis.

2. Market Research Data: Attach detailed market research findings, survey results, or any additional data supporting market analysis.

3. Product or Service Documentation: Include detailed specifications, user manuals, or any relevant documentation for products or services.

4. Legal Documents: Attach any legal documents such as contracts, permits, or licenses pertinent to the business.

5. Team Resumes: Include resumes or CVs of key team members, showcasing their qualifications and experience.

In conclusion, creating a business plan is a meticulous process that demands careful consideration of various aspects of your business. From the executive summary that captures the essence of your vision to the financial projections that outline your future, each section plays a crucial role in presenting a comprehensive picture to stakeholders. In the subsequent chapters, we will delve deeper into specific elements of business planning, offering guidance on refining strategies, implementing marketing plans, and adapting to the ever-changing business landscape.

Chapter 5
Choosing the Right Ecommerce Model

In the dynamic landscape of e-commerce, selecting the appropriate business model is a pivotal decision that shapes how you engage with customers, conduct transactions, and position your brand in the digital marketplace. This chapter navigates through the diverse types of e-commerce models, exploring their nuances and providing insights to help you make an informed choice for your business.

5.1 Types of Ecommerce Models

E-commerce models delineate the nature of transactions and the entities involved in the exchange. Understanding these models is essential for aligning your business with the right framework. Let's delve into the prominent types:

5.1.1 Business to Consumer (B2C)

B2C Overview:

Business to Consumer, or B2C, is the most common e-commerce model where businesses sell products or services directly to end consumers. This model is prevalent in online retail and encompasses a wide array of products and industries.

Key Characteristics:

1. Direct Sales: Businesses sell products or services directly to individual consumers.

2. Customer-Focused Marketing: Marketing strategies are tailored to engage and attract individual customers.

3. Mass Marketing: B2C often involves mass marketing techniques to reach a broad consumer base.

4. Single Transaction Focus: Transactions typically involve single, one-time purchases by individual customers.

Examples of B2C Businesses:

1. E-commerce Retailers: Platforms like Amazon, eBay, and Shopify facilitate direct sales to individual consumers.

2. Online Services: Streaming services, subscription boxes, and digital content providers operate under the B2C model.

5.1.2 Business to Business (B2B)

B2B Overview:
Business to Business, or B2B, involves transactions between businesses, where one entity sells products or services to another for use in their operations or resale.

Key Characteristics:

1. Wholesale Transactions: B2B transactions often involve bulk purchases at wholesale prices.

2. Longer Sales Cycles: Sales cycles in B2B are generally longer due to complex decision-making processes.

3. Relationship Building: Building strong relationships and trust is crucial in B2B transactions.

4. Customization: Products or services may be customized to meet the specific needs of the purchasing business.

Examples of B2B Businesses:

1. Manufacturers: Selling products in bulk to retailers or other manufacturers.

2. Service Providers: B2B service providers, such as marketing agencies or IT consultants, catering to businesses.

5.1.3 Consumer to Consumer (C2C)

C2C Overview:

Consumer to Consumer, or C2C, involves transactions where individual consumers sell products or services directly to other consumers. Online platforms act as intermediaries facilitating these exchanges.

Key Characteristics:

1. Peer-to-Peer Transactions: Individuals act as both sellers and buyers in direct transactions.

2. Platform Facilitation: Online marketplaces or platforms facilitate and secure C2C transactions.

3. Varied Products: C2C transactions encompass a wide range of products, including used items, handmade goods, or digital services.

4. Rating Systems: Platforms often incorporate rating systems for buyer and seller credibility.

Examples of C2C Platforms:

1. Online Marketplaces: Platforms like eBay, Craigslist, or Facebook Marketplace facilitate C2C transactions.

2. Peer-to-Peer Services: Platforms connecting individuals for services, such as Airbnb or TaskRabbit.

5.1.4 Consumer to Business (C2B)

C2B Overview:

Consumer to Business, or C2B, represents a model were individual consumers offer products or services to businesses. This model is characterized by consumers monetizing their skills, assets, or data.

Key Characteristics:

1. Individual Contributions: Individuals provide products, services, or data to businesses.

2. Freelancing and Gig Economy: C2B often involves freelancers or individuals offering services on a project basis.

3. Monetization of Data: Consumers may sell their data or insights to businesses for analysis.

4. Crowdsourcing: Businesses leverage contributions from a large number of individuals for various purposes.

Examples of C2B Transactions:

1. Freelancing Platforms: Individuals offering services on platforms like Upwork or Fiverr.

2. Data Monetization: Consumers providing data or insights to businesses for market research or product development.

5.2 Selecting the Ideal Model for Your Business

Choosing the right e-commerce model for your business requires careful consideration of various factors, including your product or service offerings, target audience, and business goals.

Decision-Making Considerations:

1. Nature of Products or Services: Consider whether your offerings are best suited for individual consumers, businesses, or peer-to-peer transactions.

2. Target Audience: Understand your target audience and their preferences, as this will influence the ideal e-commerce model.

3. Transaction Volume: Evaluate the volume and frequency of transactions your business anticipates, as different models handle transaction scales differently.

4. Marketing Strategies: Align your chosen model with the marketing strategies that resonate with your target audience.

5. Industry Dynamics: Consider industry norms and dynamics, as certain industries may naturally gravitate towards specific e-commerce models.

Strategic Planning:

1. Market Research: Conduct thorough market research to understand existing models in your industry and their success factors.

2. Competitor Analysis: Analyse competitors and their chosen e-commerce models, identifying gaps or opportunities.

3. Scalability: Assess the scalability of your chosen model to accommodate future business growth.

4. Regulatory Compliance: Consider any regulatory requirements or industry standards associated with your chosen e-commerce model.

In conclusion, choosing the right e-commerce model is a critical decision that shapes the fundamental dynamics of your business. By understanding the intricacies of B2C, B2B, C2C, and C2B models, and aligning them with your product offerings and business goals, you pave the way for a strategic and successful e-commerce venture. In the following chapters, we will delve deeper into the nuances of implementing and optimizing your chosen model, exploring strategies for effective marketing, customer engagement, and operational excellence.

Chapter 6
Building Your Online Presence

Establishing a robust online presence is a cornerstone of success in the digital realm. This chapter explores the key components of building your online presence, from choosing a domain name to designing an appealing and user-friendly ecommerce website. We'll delve into the intricacies of selecting a reliable ecommerce platform, optimizing website design, and ensuring secure payment options for a seamless customer experience.

6.1 Choosing a Domain Name

Your domain name is the digital address of your business, influencing brand perception and online visibility. Careful consideration is essential when selecting a domain name that resonates with your brand and is easy for customers to remember.

Considerations for Choosing a Domain Name:

1. Brand Alignment: Ensure the domain reflects your brand identity and is consistent with your business name.

2. Memorability: Choose a name that is easy to remember, reducing the likelihood of customers mistyping or forgetting it.

3. Keyword Relevance: If applicable, incorporate relevant keywords that align with your products or services.

4. Domain Extension: Select a domain extension (.com, .net, .org) that is widely recognized and suitable for your business type.

5. Avoid Unnecessary Complexity: Keep the domain concise, avoiding hyphens, numbers, or complex spellings.

6.2 Selecting a Reliable Ecommerce Platform

The choice of an ecommerce platform significantly influences the functionality and management of your online store. A reliable platform provides the foundation for smooth operations and optimal customer experience.

Considerations for Ecommerce Platform Selection:

1. Scalability: Choose a platform that can scale with your business growth, accommodating an increasing number of products and customers.

2. Ease of Use: Opt for a user-friendly platform that simplifies the process of product management, order fulfillment, and website customization.

3. Payment Gateway Compatibility: Ensure the platform supports popular and secure payment gateways for seamless transactions.

4. Integration Capabilities: Look for platforms that integrate with essential tools and applications, such as inventory management and analytics.

5. Mobile Responsiveness: A platform that prioritizes mobile responsiveness is crucial for catering to the growing number of mobile shoppers.

6.3 Designing Your Ecommerce Website

A visually appealing and well-designed website is the storefront of your online business. This section explores key elements of website design, emphasizing user-friendly navigation, mobile responsiveness, high-quality images, and clear product descriptions.

6.3.1 User-Friendly Navigation

Intuitive navigation is essential for guiding visitors through your website seamlessly. A well-organized structure enhances user experience and encourages exploration.

Tips for User-Friendly Navigation:

1. Clear Menu Structure: Organize your products or services into clear categories accessible through a well-structured menu.

2. Search Functionality: Implement a search bar for users to quickly find specific products or information.

3. Breadcrumb Navigation: Include breadcrumb trails to show users their location within the site hierarchy.

4. CTA Placement: Strategically place call-to-action buttons for easy access to key sections, such as the shopping cart or contact page.

6.3.2 Mobile Responsiveness

With a growing number of users accessing websites via mobile devices, ensuring mobile responsiveness is paramount. A responsive design adapts to different screen sizes, providing a consistent experience across devices.

Mobile Responsiveness Best Practices:

1. Responsive Design Framework: Utilize responsive design frameworks to ensure your website adjusts to various screen sizes.

2. Mobile-Friendly Navigation: Simplify navigation for mobile users, emphasizing easy access to essential sections.

3. Optimized Images: Compress and optimize images to enhance loading speed on mobile devices.

4. Touch-Friendly Elements: Ensure buttons and interactive elements are touch-friendly for a smooth mobile experience.

6.3.3 High-Quality Images

Visually appealing product images are fundamental in capturing the attention of online shoppers. High-quality images convey professionalism and assist customers in making informed purchasing decisions.

Guidelines for High-Quality Images:

1. Resolution and Clarity: Use images with high resolution and clarity to showcase products in detail.

2. Multiple Angles: Provide multiple images showcasing different angles and perspectives of the product.

3. Consistent Backgrounds: Maintain consistency in image backgrounds for a cohesive and professional look.

4. Zoom Functionality: Implement zoom functionality to allow users to inspect product details closely.

6.3.4 Clear Product Descriptions

Accurate and compelling product descriptions are crucial for conveying information and persuading customers to make a purchase. Clear and concise descriptions enhance the overall shopping experience.

Tips for Effective Product Descriptions:

1. Key Features: Highlight key features and specifications of each product to assist customers in making informed decisions.

2. Concise Language: Keep descriptions concise while providing enough detail for customers to understand the product.

3. Benefits Emphasis: Emphasize the benefits and unique selling points of the product to showcase its value.

4. SEO Optimization: Incorporate relevant keywords to optimize product descriptions for search engines.

6.4 Setting Up Secure Payment Options

Ensuring secure payment options is paramount for gaining customer trust and safeguarding sensitive financial information. Implementing trusted payment gateways and adhering to security standards are critical steps in this process.

Best Practices for Secure Payment Options:

1. SSL Encryption: Use SSL (Secure Sockets Layer) encryption to secure data transmission between the user's browser and your website.

2. Trusted Payment Gateways: Integrate with reputable and widely used payment gateways that prioritize security.

3. PCI DSS Compliance: Adhere to Payment Card Industry Data Security Standard (PCI DSS) compliance to safeguard credit card information.

4. Two-Factor Authentication: Implement two-factor authentication for added security during the payment process.

In conclusion, building your online presence is a multifaceted process that involves strategic decisions in domain selection, platform choice, website design, and payment security. By prioritizing user experience, mobile responsiveness, and security measures, you lay a strong foundation for attracting and retaining customers. In the following chapters, we will explore advanced strategies for marketing, customer engagement, and ongoing optimization to further enhance your online presence and drive business growth.

Chapter 7
Sourcing Products and Inventory Management

In the intricate world of e-commerce, effective product sourcing and adept inventory management are pivotal elements that can define the success and sustainability of your business. This chapter delves into the intricacies of finding reliable suppliers, determining optimal inventory levels, implementing robust inventory management systems, and ensuring stringent quality control measures.

7.1 Finding Reliable Suppliers

The foundation of a successful e-commerce venture lies in forging strong partnerships with reliable suppliers. The process of finding trustworthy suppliers involves meticulous research, due diligence, and strategic negotiations.

Strategic Supplier Sourcing:

1. Market Research: Conduct thorough market research to identify potential suppliers within your industry.

2. Industry Networks: Leverage industry networks, trade shows, and conferences to connect with reputable suppliers.

3. Online Platforms: Explore online supplier directories and platforms that connect businesses with verified suppliers.

4. Referrals and Recommendations: Seek referrals from industry peers, colleagues, or online forums for supplier recommendations.

5. Communication and Transparency: Engage in open communication with potential suppliers, assessing their responsiveness, transparency, and willingness to collaborate.

Qualities of Reliable Suppliers:

1. Reliability: Ensure suppliers have a track record of delivering quality products on time.

2. Quality Standards: Assess the adherence of suppliers to industry quality standards and certifications.

3. Capacity and Scalability: Confirm that suppliers have the capacity to meet your current and future demand.

4. Communication Skills: Effective communication with suppliers is essential for smooth collaboration and issue resolution.

5. Ethical Practices: Choose suppliers who adhere to ethical and sustainable business practices.

7.2 Determining Inventory Levels

Striking the right balance in inventory levels is a delicate art that requires consideration of demand fluctuations, lead times, and storage constraints. Effective inventory management ensures products are readily available without the burden of excess stock.

Inventory Level Determinants:

1. Sales Forecasting: Utilize historical data, market trends, and seasonality to forecast sales and plan inventory levels.

2. Lead Time: Factor in the time it takes from placing an order to receiving stock, ensuring minimal disruptions.

3. Safety Stock: Maintain a safety stock to cushion against unexpected demand spikes or delays in supply.

4. Economic Order Quantity (EOQ): Utilize EOQ models to determine optimal order quantities and minimize carrying costs.

5. ABC Analysis: Categorize products based on their importance, allocating more resources to high-value items.

7.3 Implementing Inventory Management Systems

Robust inventory management systems streamline operations, enhance accuracy, and provide real-time insights into stock levels and movement. Selecting and implementing the right system is integral to efficient inventory control.

Key Features of Inventory Management Systems:

1. Real-Time Tracking: Systems that provide real-time updates on inventory levels, preventing stockouts or overstock situations.

2. Integration with E-commerce Platform: Seamless integration with your e-commerce platform for automatic order processing and inventory updates.

3. Forecasting Tools: Utilize forecasting tools to predict demand, aiding in strategic inventory planning.

4. Barcode Scanning: Implement barcode scanning for accurate and efficient stock tracking.

5. Cloud-Based Accessibility: Opt for cloud-based systems for accessibility from various locations and scalability.

7.4 Ensuring Quality Control

Maintaining stringent quality control measures is imperative to uphold the reputation of your brand and satisfy customer expectations. From product sourcing to final delivery, every stage must adhere to established quality standards.

Comprehensive Quality Control Strategies:

1. Supplier Audits: Conduct regular audits of suppliers to ensure they adhere to quality standards and ethical practices.

2. Product Inspections: Implement thorough inspections of incoming products to identify and rectify any defects.

3. Quality Assurance Protocols: Develop and enforce robust quality assurance protocols at every stage of the supply chain.

4. Customer Feedback Analysis: Utilize customer feedback to identify potential quality issues and make continuous improvements.

5. Returns Management: Establish efficient processes for managing returns, analysing the reasons for returns, and addressing quality concerns.

Quality Control Technologies:

1. Quality Inspection Software: Implement software solutions that facilitate automated quality inspections and streamline reporting.

2. IoT and Sensors: Utilize Internet of Things (IoT) devices and sensors for real-time monitoring of product conditions.

3. Blockchain Technology: Explore blockchain technology for enhanced traceability and transparency in the supply chain.

4. Data Analytics: Leverage data analytics to identify patterns, trends, and potential quality issues in the supply chain.

In conclusion, effective sourcing of products and adept inventory management are the linchpins of a successful e-commerce operation. By meticulously selecting reliable suppliers, determining optimal inventory levels, implementing robust inventory management systems, and upholding stringent quality control measures, you lay the groundwork for a resilient and customer-centric business. In the following chapters, we will explore strategies for marketing your products, optimizing customer experiences, and adapting to the evolving landscape of e-commerce.

Chapter 8
Implementing Effective Marketing Strategies

In the ever-evolving landscape of e-commerce, the success of your online venture hinges on the effectiveness of your marketing strategies. This chapter delves into the intricacies of developing a robust marketing plan, exploring various channels and tactics to propel your brand forward. From social media marketing to building a strong brand presence and implementing customer relationship management, we unravel the key elements of driving visibility, engagement, and loyalty.

8.1 Developing a Marketing Plan

A comprehensive marketing plan serves as the guiding framework for promoting your e-commerce business. In this section, we explore the key components of a well-rounded marketing plan and delve into specific strategies across diverse channels.

8.1.1 Social Media Marketing

Social Media Marketing Overview:

Social media platforms have become indispensable channels for connecting with audiences, building brand awareness, and driving conversions. Crafting a social media strategy involves understanding the unique dynamics of each platform and tailoring your approach accordingly.

Key Strategies for Social Media Marketing:

1. Platform Selection: Identify platforms most relevant to your target audience. Platforms like Instagram and Pinterest are visual-centric, ideal for fashion or lifestyle brands, while LinkedIn may be more suitable for B2B ventures.

2. Content Calendar: Develop a content calendar to ensure consistent posting and align content with your brand messaging and promotions.

3. Engagement Strategies: Encourage audience engagement through polls, contests, and user-generated content, fostering a sense of community.

4. Influencer Collaborations: Partner with influencers whose audience aligns with your target market, leveraging their reach and credibility.

8.1.2 Content Marketing

Content Marketing Overview:

Content marketing is the strategic creation and distribution of valuable, relevant content to attract and retain a clearly defined audience. It goes beyond traditional advertising, focusing on building trust and authority.

Key Strategies for Content Marketing:

1. Content Strategy: Develop a content strategy aligned with your brand voice and values, catering to the informational needs and preferences of your audience.

2. Blogging: Maintain a blog to showcase industry expertise, share product insights, and improve SEO through relevant keywords.

3. Video Content: Leverage the power of video content, whether through product tutorials, behind-the-scenes glimpses, or engaging storytelling.

4. Ebooks and Guides: Create in-depth ebooks or guides that provide value to your audience while establishing your brand as an authoritative source.

8.1.3 Influencer Marketing

Influencer Marketing Overview:

Influencer marketing involves partnering with individuals who have a significant following and impact within your target audience. Their endorsement can enhance brand credibility and expand your reach.

Key Strategies for Influencer Marketing:

1. Identifying Relevant Influencers: Research and identify influencers whose values and audience align with your brand.

2. Authentic Partnerships: Foster authentic partnerships by allowing influencers creative freedom and ensuring the collaboration aligns with their personal brand.

3. Measuring Impact: Use tracking tools and metrics to measure the impact of influencer campaigns, evaluating reach, engagement, and conversion rates.

4. Long-Term Relationships: Cultivate long-term relationships with influencers for ongoing collaborations, establishing brand consistency.

8.1.4 Email Marketing

Email Marketing Overview:

Email marketing remains a powerful tool for engaging with your audience, nurturing leads, and driving sales. Crafting compelling email campaigns involves strategic planning and understanding your audience's preferences.

Key Strategies for Email Marketing:

1. Segmentation: Segment your email list based on demographics, purchasing behaviour, or engagement levels, allowing for targeted and personalized campaigns.

2. Automation: Implement automation for welcome emails, abandoned cart reminders, and post-purchase follow-ups, streamlining communication.

3. Personalization: Personalize email content, addressing recipients by name and tailoring recommendations based on their preferences.

4. A/B Testing: Conduct A/B testing for subject lines, content, and visuals, refining your approach based on data-driven insights.

8.1.5 Search Engine Optimization (SEO)

SEO Overview:

Search Engine Optimization is fundamental for improving your website's visibility in search engine results. A well-optimized site attracts organic traffic and enhances the overall user experience.

Key Strategies for SEO:

1. Keyword Research: Conduct thorough keyword research to identify relevant search terms and phrases for your industry.

2. On-Page Optimization: Optimize meta titles, descriptions, and headers with target keywords, improving the site's overall search engine friendliness.

3. Quality Content: Create high-quality, valuable content that aligns with user intent, solving problems or providing relevant information.

4. Link Building: Build backlinks from reputable sources, as they contribute to your site's authority and search engine rankings.

8.1.6 Paid Advertising

Paid Advertising Overview:

Paid advertising provides a direct and immediate way to drive traffic and conversions. Platforms like Google Ads and social media advertising allow for targeted campaigns based on demographics, interests, and behaviours.

Key Strategies for Paid Advertising:

1. Target Audience Selection: Define and refine your target audience to ensure your ads reach the most relevant users.

2. Compelling Ad Copy: Craft compelling ad copy that communicates your unique selling propositions and encourages action.

3. Visual Appeal: Design visually appealing ads that align with your brand identity and capture attention.

4. Budget Management: Set realistic budgets, monitor ad performance, and adjust spending based on campaign success.

8.2 Building a Strong Brand Presence

Brand Presence Overview:

A strong brand presence is essential for standing out in the crowded digital landscape. It encompasses brand identity, values, and the emotional connection you establish with your audience.

Key Strategies for Building a Strong Brand Presence:

1. Consistent Branding: Maintain consistency in visual elements, messaging, and tone across all channels, fostering brand recognition.

2. Storytelling: Craft a compelling brand story that resonates with your audience, creating an emotional connection.

3. Customer Reviews and Testimonials: Showcase positive customer reviews and testimonials to build trust and credibility.

4. Community Engagement: Engage with your audience on social media, responding to comments, participating in discussions, and creating a sense of community.

8.3 Customer Relationship Management (CRM)

CRM Overview:

Customer Relationship Management is about nurturing and managing relationships with your customers. It involves understanding their needs, preferences, and interactions with your brand.

Key Strategies for CRM:

1. Customer Segmentation: Segment your customer base based on behaviour, preferences, or demographics, allowing for targeted communication.

2. Personalized Communication: Leverage data to personalize communications, tailoring offers, and recommendations to individual customers.

3. Feedback and Surveys: Solicit feedback through surveys and reviews, demonstrating a commitment to customer satisfaction and continuous improvement.

4. Loyalty Programs: Implement loyalty programs to reward repeat customers, fostering brand loyalty and retention.

In conclusion, implementing effective marketing strategies requires a holistic approach that encompasses diverse channels and tactics. By developing a comprehensive marketing plan, leveraging social media, content marketing, influencer collaborations, email campaigns, SEO, and paid advertising, you create a multi-faceted approach to reach and engage your target audience. Additionally, building a strong brand presence and implementing customer relationship management practices contribute to long-term success and customer loyalty. In the following chapters, we will delve into operational aspects, including product sourcing, inventory management, and further strategies to enhance your e-commerce venture.

Chapter 9
Ensuring Legal Compliance

Navigating the legal landscape is crucial for the success and sustainability of your e-commerce venture. This chapter explores the key aspects of ensuring legal compliance, from registering your business to understanding taxation, complying with e-commerce regulations, and protecting intellectual property.

9.1 Registering Your Business

Business Registration Overview:

Registering your business is a foundational step that establishes your legal identity, ensures compliance with regulations, and provides a framework for operations.

Key Considerations for Business Registration:

1. Legal Structure Selection: Choose a legal structure that aligns with your business goals, such as sole proprietorship, LLC, or corporation.

2. Business Name Registration: Register a unique and legally compliant business name, considering trademarks and domain availability.

3. State and Federal Registrations: Fulfill state-specific registration requirements and consider federal registrations if operating across state lines.

4. Tax Identification Number (TIN): Obtain a TIN from the IRS for tax reporting purposes.

Benefits of Business Registration:

1. Legal Recognition: Registration provides legal recognition of your business entity, distinguishing it from personal assets.

2. Access to Business Services: Registered businesses gain access to various business services, including banking, loans, and vendor relationships.

3. Legal Protections: Certain legal structures offer liability protection, shielding personal assets from business-related liabilities.

9.2 Understanding Taxation

Taxation Overview:

Understanding taxation is essential for managing financial obligations, meeting compliance requirements, and optimizing your business's financial health.

Key Considerations for Understanding Taxation:

1. Tax Structure Selection: Choose a tax structure that aligns with your business type, such as sole proprietorship, partnership, corporation, or S-corporation.

2. Sales Tax Compliance: Comply with state and local sales tax regulations, including collection, reporting, and remittance.

3. Income Tax Obligations: Fulfill federal and state income tax obligations, considering deductions, credits, and filing deadlines.

4. Tax Professionals: Consider engaging tax professionals for guidance on complex tax matters and to ensure compliance with evolving tax laws.

Benefits of Understanding Taxation:

1. Financial Planning: A clear understanding of taxation allows for strategic financial planning, minimizing tax liabilities and maximizing deductions.

2. Compliance Assurance: Compliance with tax regulations ensures legal adherence and avoids penalties or legal repercussions.

3. Optimized Financial Performance: Proper tax management contributes to optimized financial performance and sustainable business growth.

9.3 Complying with E-commerce Regulations

E-commerce Regulations Overview:
Compliance with e-commerce regulations is essential for building trust with customers, avoiding legal issues, and maintaining a secure online environment.

Key Considerations for E-commerce Regulations:

1. Privacy Policies: Develop and prominently display a privacy policy outlining how customer data is collected, used, and protected.

2. Terms and Conditions: Clearly define terms and conditions governing transactions, returns, and disputes to manage customer expectations.

3. Data Security: Implement robust data security measures to protect customer information from unauthorized access or breaches.

4. Consumer Protection Laws: Adhere to consumer protection laws, including transparent pricing, accurate product information, and fair business practices.

Benefits of E-commerce Regulations Compliance:

1. Customer Trust: Demonstrating compliance builds trust with customers, assuring them of a secure and ethical online shopping experience.

2. Legal Protection: Compliance safeguards your business from legal disputes, regulatory fines, and reputational damage.

3. Competitive Advantage: E-commerce businesses that prioritize compliance gain a competitive edge, attracting conscious consumers.

9.4 Protecting Intellectual Property

Intellectual Property Protection Overview:

Intellectual property includes trademarks, copyrights, patents, and trade secrets. Protecting these assets is vital for safeguarding your brand and innovations.

Key Considerations for Intellectual Property Protection:

1. Trademark Registration: Register trademarks for business names, logos, and product names to prevent unauthorized use by competitors.

2. Copyright Protection: Secure copyright for original content, such as website text, images, and multimedia, to prevent unauthorized reproduction.

3. Patent Filings: If applicable, explore patent filings to protect unique inventions, designs, or processes associated with your products.

4. Trade Secret Safeguards: Implement measures to safeguard trade secrets, such as proprietary formulas or business processes.

Benefits of Intellectual Property Protection:

1. Brand Integrity: Protection of trademarks ensures the integrity of your brand, preventing confusion or misuse in the market.

2. Market Exclusivity: Securing patents provides exclusive rights, allowing you to capitalize on innovations without direct competition.

3. Legal Recourse: Intellectual property protection provides legal recourse in case of infringement, enabling you to defend your assets.

In conclusion, ensuring legal compliance is a foundational aspect of building and maintaining a successful e-commerce business. From registering your business and understanding taxation to complying with e-commerce regulations and protecting intellectual property, these measures contribute to legal adherence, financial stability, and brand integrity. In the subsequent chapters, we will explore operational aspects, including product sourcing, inventory management, and marketing strategies for sustained success in the competitive e-commerce landscape.

Chapter 10
Scaling Your Ecommerce Business

In the dynamic realm of e-commerce, the journey doesn't end with the establishment of an online presence; it's about continuous evolution and strategic scaling. This chapter explores the multifaceted strategies involved in scaling your e-commerce business, emphasizing the critical importance of analysing performance metrics, expanding product lines, exploring new markets, enhancing customer experience, and investing in technology and automation.

10.1 Analysing Performance Metrics

As the adage goes, "what gets measured gets managed." In the context of e-commerce, understanding and analysing performance metrics are pivotal for informed decision-making and sustained growth.

Strategic Importance of Performance Metrics:

Effective performance analysis involves a comprehensive examination of key performance indicators (KPIs), traffic sources, customer acquisition cost, conversion rates, and more. These metrics offer invaluable insights into the health and efficiency of your e-commerce operations.

Key Components of Analysing Performance Metrics:

1. Conversion Rates: Evaluate the effectiveness of your sales funnel by analysing conversion rates at different stages. Identify points of friction and optimize the user journey for enhanced conversions.

2. Average Order Value (AOV): Understand the average amount spent by customers per transaction. Strategies for upselling and cross-selling can be refined based on AOV insights.

3. Customer Acquisition Cost (CAC): Calculate the cost of acquiring a new customer, comparing it to the customer's lifetime value (CLV) for a comprehensive view of marketing ROI.

4. Traffic Sources: Identify the sources of website traffic, distinguishing between organic, paid, and referral sources. Allocate resources based on the most effective channels.

5. Customer Retention Metrics: Measure customer retention rates, repeat purchase frequency, and overall customer loyalty. Implement strategies to nurture long-term relationships.

Data-Driven Decision-Making:

1. Advanced Analytics Tools: Employ advanced analytics tools such as Google Analytics, heatmaps, and user behaviour tracking to gather granular insights.

2. A/B Testing: Conduct A/B testing on various elements, including website design, product pages, and marketing campaigns, using data-driven results for continuous improvement.

3. Customer Feedback: Actively seek and analyse customer feedback through surveys and reviews, incorporating valuable insights into strategic decisions.

10.2 Expanding Product Lines

A key driver of e-commerce growth lies in the strategic expansion of product lines. This involves not only introducing new products but also optimizing existing offerings for maximum impact.

Strategies for Product Expansion:

1. Market Research: Conduct thorough market research to identify emerging trends, gaps in the market, and customer preferences. Leverage data to inform product development decisions.

2. Diversification: Introduce complementary products or variations to cater to a broader customer base. This not only increases the breadth of offerings but also enhances cross-selling opportunities.

3. Seasonal Offerings: Strategically introduce seasonal or limited-edition products to create a sense of urgency and excitement, driving both new and repeat purchases.

4. Cross-Selling and Upselling: Implement cross-selling and upselling strategies to increase the average order value and improve overall revenue per customer.

Product Lifecycle Management:

1. Product Life Cycle Analysis: Regularly evaluate the life cycle of existing products. Plan for product refreshes, updates, or discontinuations based on performance and market dynamics.

2. Inventory Management: Optimize inventory levels to accommodate new product introductions while preventing overstock or stockouts.

10.3 Exploring New Markets

For sustained growth, venturing into new markets can unlock untapped potential. However, this expansion requires a nuanced approach and careful consideration of diverse factors.

Strategic Approaches to Market Expansion:

1. Global Market Research: Conduct comprehensive research to identify viable international markets. Consider cultural nuances, demand patterns, and competition.

2. Localization: Adapt marketing strategies, product offerings, and website content to cater to the preferences and languages of the target market. This ensures a seamless and culturally relevant customer experience.

3. Partnerships and Alliances: Explore strategic partnerships or alliances with local distributors, retailers, or e-commerce platforms. This can facilitate smoother market entry by leveraging established networks.

Evaluating Market Entry Strategies:

1. E-commerce Platforms: Leverage established global e-commerce platforms to reach a wider audience without the complexities of setting up a physical presence.

2. Local Warehousing and Fulfillment: Consider establishing local warehousing and fulfillment centres to optimize shipping times and costs. This enhances the overall customer experience.

3. Regulatory Compliance: Ensure meticulous compliance with international regulations, customs requirements, and tax considerations for seamless cross-border operations.

10.4 Enhancing Customer Experience

A superior customer experience is a cornerstone of successful e-commerce businesses. As you scale, prioritizing and continually enhancing the customer journey becomes even more critical.

Strategies for Superior Customer Experience:

1. User-Friendly Website: Continuously optimize the website for easy navigation, intuitive design, and seamless transactions. Regularly update the user interface based on user behaviour and feedback.

2. Personalization: Implement personalized product recommendations, tailored promotions, and targeted communications based on individual customer preferences and behaviour.

3. Responsive Customer Support: Provide responsive and multi-channel customer support. Address queries, concerns, and feedback promptly to foster positive customer interactions.

4. Streamlined Checkout Process: Simplify the checkout process to minimize friction and reduce cart abandonment rates. Implement features such as guest checkout and one-click purchasing for convenience.

5. Loyalty Programs: Introduce and enhance loyalty programs to reward repeat customers. Loyalty programs foster engagement, encourage repeat purchases, and contribute to brand advocacy.

Customer Feedback and Iterative Improvement:

1. Feedback Loops: Establish effective feedback loops through customer surveys, reviews, and social media interactions. Leverage this feedback to identify areas for improvement and implement iterative changes.

2. Iterative Testing: Continuously test website features, user interfaces, and customer communication strategies based on real-time feedback and data. This iterative approach ensures ongoing optimization.

10.5 Investing in Technology and Automation

As your e-commerce business scales, leveraging technology and automation becomes instrumental for maintaining operational efficiency, enhancing customer experiences, and staying ahead in a competitive landscape.

Strategic Technology Investments:

1. E-commerce Platforms: Regularly evaluate and, if necessary, upgrade your e-commerce platform to accommodate growth, scalability, and evolving technological trends. Ensure the platform aligns with your long-term business goals.

2. Automation Tools: Implement automation tools for key business processes, such as order processing, inventory management, and customer communication. Automation enhances efficiency and reduces manual workload.

3. Data Security: Prioritize robust cybersecurity measures to safeguard customer data, financial transactions, and sensitive business information. Building and maintaining trust is crucial for long-term success.

Emerging Technologies:

1. Artificial Intelligence (AI): Explore applications of AI for personalized product recommendations, chatbots for customer support, and predictive analytics for inventory management.

2. Augmented Reality (AR) and Virtual Reality (VR):
Consider integrating AR and VR technologies for immersive product experiences and virtual try-ons. This enhances the online shopping experience.

3. Blockchain: Explore blockchain technology for transparent and secure supply chain management. Blockchain can be used to verify product authenticity, reducing fraud and increasing customer trust.

In conclusion, scaling your e-commerce business is a multifaceted journey that demands strategic vision and adaptability. By diligently analysing performance metrics, expanding product lines, exploring new markets, enhancing customer experience, and investing in technology and automation, you position your business for sustained growth and competitiveness. The subsequent chapters will delve into legal compliance considerations and conclude with a comprehensive overview of the e-commerce journey.

Chapter 11
Case Studies

In the world of e-commerce, success stories and lessons learned from real-life experiences can be powerful sources of inspiration and guidance. This chapter delves into a series of case studies that highlight the diverse journeys, challenges, and triumphs of e-commerce businesses. These cases span various industries, showcasing the adaptability and innovation required for sustained success in the dynamic digital marketplace.

Case Study 1: From Local to Global - The Rise of a Niche Artisanal Brand

Background:
In this case study, we explore the journey of a small artisanal brand that started as a local business crafting handmade product. Through strategic online positioning, targeted marketing, and leveraging e-commerce platforms, the brand successfully expanded its reach from a local market to a global audience.

Key Takeaways:

1. Niche Branding: The importance of niche branding and storytelling in capturing the attention of a global audience.

2. E-commerce Platform Selection: The role of selecting the right e-commerce platforms in reaching a wider market and managing international transactions.

3. Digital Marketing Strategies: How targeted digital marketing strategies, including social media and influencer collaborations, played a pivotal role in global brand awareness.

Case Study 2: From Brick-and-Mortar to E-commerce Dominance - A Legacy Retailer's Transformation

Background:
This case study explores the transformation journey of a traditional brick-and-mortar retailer faced with the challenges of a changing retail landscape. The retailer successfully navigated the shift to e-commerce, embracing omnichannel strategies to maintain a strong market presence.

Key Takeaways:

1. Omnichannel Integration: The importance of seamlessly integrating online and offline channels to provide a cohesive customer experience.

2. Customer Loyalty Programs: Strategies for retaining and transitioning loyal customers from physical stores to online platforms.

3. Adaptability and Innovation: How a legacy retailer embraced technological advancements, including mobile apps and augmented reality, to stay competitive in the digital era.

Case Study 3: Disrupting the Market - A Start-up's Journey to E-commerce Dominance

Background:
This case study follows the journey of a disruptive start-up that entered a saturated market and quickly gained prominence through innovative e-commerce strategies. From guerrilla marketing tactics to leveraging user-generated content, the start-up disrupted traditional industry norms.

Key Takeaways:

1. Guerrilla Marketing: The role of unconventional marketing strategies in creating buzz and standing out in a competitive landscape.

2. User-Generated Content: Harnessing the power of user-generated content for authentic brand promotion and community building.

3. Agile Business Models: The significance of agile business models that can quickly adapt to market changes and capitalize on emerging trends.

Case Study 4: Adapting to Crisis - The Resilience of an E-commerce Giant

Background:
This case study examines how a prominent e-commerce giant navigated and adapted to unforeseen challenges, such as economic downturns, supply chain disruptions, and global

crises. It highlights the resilience and strategic decisions that allowed the company to not only survive but thrive in the face of adversity.

Key Takeaways:

1. Strategic Diversification: The importance of diversifying product offerings and revenue streams to mitigate risks during economic uncertainties.

2. Supply Chain Agility: How having a flexible and agile supply chain contributed to overcoming disruptions and maintaining customer satisfaction.

3. Customer-Centric Approach: The role of a customer-centric approach, including transparent communication and support, in building trust during challenging times.

Case Study 5: Sustainability in E-commerce - A Green Marketplace's Success Story

Background:
This case study explores the success story of an e-commerce platform dedicated to sustainable and eco-friendly products. It delves into how the platform curated a marketplace that resonated with environmentally conscious consumers and contributed to the broader sustainability movement.

Key Takeaways:

1. Purpose-Driven Branding: The significance of aligning the brand with a purpose, such as sustainability, to attract a specific target audience.

2. Supplier Standards: The role of implementing stringent supplier standards to ensure the authenticity and environmental impact of products.

3. Educational Marketing: How educational content and marketing initiatives played a crucial role in raising awareness about sustainable practices among consumers.

Case Study 6: The Power of Personalization - A Customization-Focused E-commerce Venture

Background:
This case study delves into the journey of an e-commerce venture that placed a strong emphasis on personalization and customization. By offering tailored products and experiences, the brand created a loyal customer base and distinguished itself in a competitive market.

Key Takeaways:

1. Personalized Shopping Experiences: The impact of providing personalized product recommendations, customized offerings, and interactive shopping experiences.

2. Data-Driven Personalization: The role of data analytics in understanding customer preferences and tailoring marketing strategies and product offerings accordingly.

3. Customer Engagement: How fostering a sense of community and engagement through personalized interactions contributed to brand loyalty.

Conclusion: Drawing Insights from Diverse Journeys

In conclusion, these case studies illuminate the diverse paths that e-commerce businesses can take to achieve success. Whether through niche branding, omnichannel strategies, disruptive innovation, resilience in times of crisis, sustainability initiatives, or the power of personalization, each case offers valuable insights and lessons for aspiring and established e-commerce entrepreneurs. As we wrap up this chapter, the collective wisdom drawn from these case studies serves as a source of inspiration and strategic guidance for navigating the ever-evolving landscape of e-commerce.

Chapter 12
Conclusion

Embarking on the journey of e-commerce is a thrilling adventure marked by continuous learning, adaptation, and growth. Throughout this comprehensive guide, we have navigated the intricacies of establishing, managing, and scaling an e-commerce business. As we conclude, let's recap the key takeaways and set our sights on the future of e-commerce.

Recap of Key Takeaways:

1. Understanding Ecommerce:

- Ecommerce encompasses a diverse range of online business models, from traditional retail to dropshipping and beyond.

- The advantages and disadvantages of e-commerce must be carefully considered, weighing factors such as cost, convenience, and market dynamics.

2. Finding Your Niche:

- Identifying a niche that aligns with your passion, expertise, and market demand is crucial for long-term success.

- Thorough research into market demand, competitor analysis, and personal interests aids in niche selection.

3. Market Research and Validation:

- Conducting market research, defining target audiences, and validating product or service ideas are foundational steps in building a successful e-commerce venture.

- Refining business ideas based on market feedback and continuously iterating on products and strategies is essential.

4. Creating a Business Plan:

- A well-crafted business plan serves as a roadmap, outlining key components such as executive summaries, market analyses, and financial projections.

- Regularly revisiting and adjusting the business plan ensures alignment with evolving market trends and business goals.

5. Choosing the Right Ecommerce Model:

- Selecting the appropriate e-commerce model, whether B2C, B2B, C2C, or C2B, depends on the nature of your products or services.

- Understanding the nuances of each model helps in tailoring your approach to the target audience.

6. Building Your Online Presence:

- Choosing a domain name, selecting a reliable e-commerce platform, and designing a user-friendly website are critical for establishing a strong online presence.

- Implementing secure payment options and responsive design contributes to a positive user experience.

7. Sourcing Products and Inventory Management:

- Finding reliable suppliers, determining optimal inventory levels, and implementing robust inventory management systems are vital for smooth operations.

- Quality control measures ensure that products meet or exceed customer expectations.

8. Implementing Effective Marketing Strategies:

- Developing a marketing plan that includes social media marketing, content marketing, influencer collaborations, email marketing, SEO, and paid advertising is essential for visibility.

- Building a strong brand presence and implementing customer relationship management practices contribute to long-term success.

9. Ensuring Legal Compliance:

- Registering the business, understanding taxation, complying with e-commerce regulations, and protecting intellectual property are crucial for legal compliance.

- Adhering to ethical business practices builds trust and credibility with customers and stakeholders.

10. Scaling Your Ecommerce Business:

- Analyzing performance metrics, expanding product lines, exploring new markets, enhancing customer experience, and investing in technology and automation drive sustained growth.

- Careful evaluation of market dynamics and strategic decision-making are essential components of successful scaling.

11. Case Studies:

- Exploring case studies of both successful e-commerce ventures and learning from failures provides valuable insights and lessons for aspiring entrepreneurs.

12. Conclusion:

- The journey of e-commerce is dynamic, requiring adaptability, resilience, and a commitment to continuous improvement.

- By staying informed about industry trends, embracing emerging technologies, and fostering a customer-centric approach, e-commerce businesses can thrive in an ever-evolving landscape.

Embracing the Future of Ecommerce:

The future of e-commerce holds exciting possibilities as technology continues to evolve, consumer preferences shift, and global markets become more interconnected. To stay ahead, e-commerce entrepreneurs should consider:

1. Embracing Emerging Technologies:

- Explore innovations such as artificial intelligence, augmented reality, and blockchain to enhance the customer experience and operational efficiency.

- Adopting cutting-edge technologies can set your e-commerce business apart and position it for future success.

2. Adapting to Changing Consumer Behaviours:

- Keep a pulse on evolving consumer behaviours and preferences. Understanding shifts in how customers shop and interact online is crucial for staying relevant.

3. Focusing on Sustainability:

- With growing environmental awareness, incorporating sustainable practices in product sourcing, packaging, and operations can resonate with eco-conscious consumers.

4. Global Expansion Opportunities:

- Consider expanding into new international markets, leveraging the global reach of e-commerce platforms and strategic partnerships.

- Adapting to diverse cultural contexts and regulatory environments is key for successful international expansion.

5. Continuous Learning and Innovation:

- The e-commerce landscape is dynamic, with new trends and technologies emerging regularly. Commit to continuous learning, staying informed about industry developments, and fostering a culture of innovation.

In conclusion, the world of e-commerce offers boundless opportunities for those willing to navigate its challenges and seize its potential. As you embark on or continue your e-commerce journey, remember that success is often a result of strategic planning, relentless dedication, and a customer-centric mindset. The future of e-commerce is bright, and your role as an entrepreneur is to shape it through innovation, resilience, and a commitment to excellence.

Appendix: Resources and Tools

In the fast-paced world of e-commerce, staying equipped with the right resources and tools is essential for success. This comprehensive guide in the appendix provides an in-depth exploration of the myriad resources available to e-commerce entrepreneurs, along with an extensive glossary of essential terms to enhance understanding.

1. E-commerce Platforms: Choosing the Right Foundation

Selecting the appropriate e-commerce platform is a critical decision that shapes the foundation of your online business. Explore popular platforms such as Shopify, WooCommerce, Magento, and BigCommerce. Understand the features, pricing models, and scalability of each to make an informed choice aligned with your business goals.

2. Website Design and Development Tools: Crafting an Engaging Online Presence

Building a user-friendly and visually appealing website is paramount for e-commerce success. Dive into tools like WordPress, Squarespace, and Wix for website development. Explore design tools like Canva and Adobe Spark for creating captivating visuals that resonate with your brand identity.

3. Payment Gateways: Ensuring Secure Transactions

Discover the world of payment gateways and explore options such as PayPal, Stripe, and Square. Delve into their features, transaction fees, and integration capabilities to provide seamless and secure payment experiences for your customers.

4. Inventory Management Tools: Streamlining Operations

Efficient inventory management is crucial for preventing stockouts and overstock situations. Learn about tools like TradeGecko, Zoho Inventory, and DEAR Inventory, which offer functionalities for inventory tracking, order fulfillment, and demand forecasting.

5. Shipping and Fulfillment Solutions: Delivering Excellence

Explore shipping and fulfillment solutions such as ShipStation, Shippo, and Easyship. Understand how these platforms streamline the shipping process, provide real-time shipping rates, and offer insights into cost-effective delivery options.

6. Marketing and SEO Tools: Driving Visibility and Engagement

Effective marketing is the lifeblood of e-commerce. Uncover tools like Mailchimp, HubSpot, and SEMrush for email marketing, content creation, and SEO optimization. Learn how these tools can elevate your marketing strategies and enhance your online presence.

7. Customer Support and Communication Tools: Building Trust

Exceptional customer support is a cornerstone of successful e-commerce ventures. Explore tools like Zendesk, Freshdesk, and LiveChat for efficient communication, ticket management, and creating positive customer experiences.

8. Analytics and Reporting Tools: Harnessing Data for Growth

Data-driven decision-making is integral to scaling your e-commerce business. Discover analytics tools like Google Analytics, Hotjar, and Crazy Egg for gaining insights into user behaviour, website performance, and conversion rates.

9. Social Media Management Tools: Amplifying Your Reach

Social media plays a pivotal role in e-commerce marketing. Explore tools like Hootsuite, Buffer, and Sprout Social for managing multiple social media accounts, scheduling posts, and analysing engagement metrics.

10. E-commerce Communities and Forums: Connecting with Peers

Engaging with the e-commerce community is invaluable for learning, networking, and seeking advice. Explore forums like Shopify Community, eCommerceFuel, and BigCommerce Community to connect with fellow entrepreneurs, share experiences, and gain valuable insights.

Glossary of E-commerce Terms

To navigate the intricate landscape of e-commerce, understanding industry-specific terminology is essential. This glossary provides clarity on commonly used terms, acronyms, and concepts within the e-commerce realm.

Appendix: Resources and Tools, Glossary of Ecommerce Terms

Resources and Tools:

E-commerce entrepreneurs can benefit from a plethora of resources and tools to streamline operations, enhance marketing efforts, and stay informed about industry trends. Some essential resources include:

1. E-commerce Platforms:
   - Shopify
   - WooCommerce
   - Magento

2. Marketing Tools:
- Google Analytics
- Mailchimp
- Hootsuite

3. Inventory Management:
- TradeGecko
- Skubana
- Zoho Inventory

4. Legal Compliance:
- LegalZoom
- TermsFeed
- Shopify Legal Guides

5. Financial Tools:
- QuickBooks
- Xero
- Wave

Glossary of Ecommerce Terms:

Understanding the terminology of e-commerce is essential for effective communication within the industry. Here's a comprehensive glossary of commonly used terms:

1. B2B (Business to Business): Commerce transactions between businesses.

2. B2C (Business to Consumer): Commerce transactions between a business and individual consumer.

3. C2C (Consumer to Consumer): Commerce transactions between individual consumers.

4. C2B (Consumer to Business): Commerce transactions where consumers sell products or services to businesses.

5. Dropshipping: A retail fulfillment method where a store doesn't keep the products it sells in stock, relying on third-party suppliers to fulfill orders.

6. Conversion Rate: The percentage of website visitors who complete a desired action, such as making a purchase.

7. SEO (Search Engine Optimization): The practice of optimizing online content to rank higher in search engine results.

8. CRM (Customer Relationship Management): Strategies and technologies used to manage and analyse customer interactions.

9. KPIs (Key Performance Indicators): Specific metrics used to evaluate the success of an organization or particular activity.

10. ROI (Return on Investment): A measure of the profitability of an investment, calculated as the ratio of net profit to the initial cost.

Understanding and utilizing

these resources and terms will empower e-commerce entrepreneurs to navigate the complex landscape, make informed decisions, and contribute to the overall success of their ventures.

In closing, the journey of e-commerce is a dynamic and rewarding venture that requires dedication, strategic thinking, and a passion for innovation. Whether you're just starting or scaling your business, the principles outlined in this guide serve as a valuable compass. As you navigate the ever-changing e-commerce landscape, may your entrepreneurial spirit remain undaunted, and your success stories be plentiful. Best of luck on your e-commerce journey!

Chapter 13
20 niche ideas for an ecommerce business

1. Sustainable and Eco-Friendly Products:

- Cater to the growing demand for environmentally conscious consumers by offering sustainable and eco-friendly products, such as reusable goods, organic clothing, or zero-waste essentials.

2. Personalized Pet Products:

- Create a niche by offering personalized pet accessories, from custom pet collars to engraved feeding bowls, catering to the pet-loving demographic.

3. Customized Fitness Equipment:

- Appeal to fitness enthusiasts by offering customized workout gear, such as personalized dumbbells, yoga mats, or fitness apparel.

4. Smart Home Devices:

- Capitalize on the smart home trend by curating a collection of innovative and connected devices, ranging from smart lighting to home automation kits.

5. Educational Toys and Games:

- Target parents and educators by offering a curated selection of educational toys and games for children, emphasizing both fun and learning.

6. Ethnic and Handmade Jewellery:

- Showcase unique and handmade jewellery from different cultures, offering customers a diverse range of ethnic and culturally rich accessories.

7. Plant-Based Foods and Snacks:

- Tap into the growing market of health-conscious consumers by offering a variety of plant-based and vegan foods, snacks, and beverages.

8. Personal Safety and Security Products:

- Address the need for personal safety with a range of security products, such as personal alarms, self-defence tools, and safety wearables.

9. Subscription-Box for Hobbies:

- Curate subscription boxes tailored to specific hobbies or interests, such as art supplies, gardening tools, or DIY crafting kits.

10. Vintage and Retro Clothing:

- Create a niche in the fashion industry by offering curated collections of vintage and retro clothing, appealing to those with a love for timeless styles.

11. Tech Accessories for Remote Work:

- Cater to the remote workforce by providing innovative and ergonomic tech accessories, such as laptop stands, noise-cancelling headphones, and ergonomic keyboards.

12. Natural Beauty and Skincare:

- Offer a selection of natural and organic beauty products, emphasizing clean ingredients and sustainable packaging to cater to the health-conscious consumer.

13. Personal Finance and Budgeting Tools:

- Address the need for financial management by offering tools, planners, and resources focused on personal finance and budgeting.

14. Subscription-Box for Book Lovers:

- Create subscription boxes tailored to avid readers, including curated book selections, author-themed merchandise, and reading accessories.

15. Smartphone Accessories for Travel:

- Target travellers by offering a range of innovative smartphone accessories designed for convenience during travel, such as portable chargers, travel-friendly phone stands, and camera attachments.

16. Gourmet Cooking Ingredients:

- Appeal to food enthusiasts by offering high-quality and unique gourmet cooking ingredients, such as rare spices, infused oils, or specialty sauces.

17. Customized Home Office Furniture:

- Cater to the increasing number of remote workers by providing customized and ergonomic home office furniture, ranging from desks to ergonomic chairs.

18. DIY Home Improvement Kits:

- Target homeowners with DIY home improvement kits, providing everything needed for a specific project, such as painting, gardening, or furniture assembly.

19. Mindfulness and Meditation Products:

- Tap into the wellness trend by offering mindfulness and meditation products, including meditation cushions, aromatherapy kits, and guided meditation resources.

20. Outdoor Adventure Gear:

- Serve outdoor enthusiasts by offering a curated collection of adventure gear, from camping essentials to hiking accessories, catering to the active lifestyle.

When choosing a niche, consider your own interests, market trends, and the needs of your target audience. A successful ecommerce business often combines passion with market demand.

 official.factsofworth@gmail.com

im_deepak.prajapati

THANK YOU......

www.ingramcontent.com/pod-product-compliance
Lightning Source LLC
Chambersburg PA
CBHW071057290526
45795CB00004B/1542